To Ruth,

Thank you for the inspiration
and the joy for the journey.

Lorraine Dahlem Tufts
1/31/97
Delray Bch, Fl.

Animals in Action
by
Lorraine Salem Tufts

Photographs by Lorraine Salem Tufts
Designer: Lorraine Salem Tufts
Editor: Tracey Ingraham Holmes
Assistant Editor: Jules Dowler

Printed by Palace Press—China
Hardcover: First Edition T
1 2 3 4 5 6 7 8 9 10
Library of Congress Cataloging in Publication Data
Tufts, Lorraine Salem   1947-
Animals in Action
1. Animals—Description—Photographic
2. Wildlife—Nature
I. Tufts, Lorraine Salem   II. Title
. . 1995   •   95-92224
Action #1
ISBN 09620255-5-0-HC

Dedication

Pine Jog Environmental Center for Children
and
Dedicated teachers and librarians
so often the unsung heroes in society.

Robin Chicks

Robins build sturdy nests of mud, grass and twigs for their eggs. Newborn robins stretch up their heads for food. Both parents hunt for insects, worms and berries to feed their chicks.

Grizzly Bears

The large, female grizzly bear points her nose to the wind, sniffing for any sign of trouble. All seems safe for her and her little cub at this moment. It is a cold and rainy morning, but she and her little one are warm in their natural fur.

Mother grizzly bear looks for fish in a small stream. The cub, who is about four months old, learns to fish and survive

by watching his mother. Female grizzlies are extremely protective of their cubs.

Mother grizzly bears are the great teachers of life to their young. Offspring will stay close to their mothers for about two years, before starting life on their own. Grizzly bears are an endangered species.

Brown Pelican

Watching this brown pelican fly along the water is a beautiful sight, even for this funny faced bird. Breeding adults have bright colors, while only the first- and second-year immatures are brown. Brown pelicans are quite large, but generally not as big as the white pelican.

Brown pelicans are masters of flight and will dive in unison with other pelicans for fish. These pelicans will fly together, change direction and then dive all at the same time. Often the pelicans will come up with fish. This is an amazing feat of animal cooperation and great fun to watch. Brown pelicans are an endangered species.

River Otters

River otters are fast and graceful swimmers. They are also skillful divers, capable of staying underwater for as long as five minutes. They mainly catch and eat fish, but will also eat insects, frogs and water animals with a shell.

Females will call their young to join them in the water only 10 to 12 weeks after birth. If one resists, the mother picks up the protesting pup and plops it in the water. The following weeks are spent giving swimming lessons. Otter pups are also given lessons on capturing live prey such as fish. River otters generally live a playful life of about eleven years.

Great Blue Heron

The great blue heron is the most widespread heron in all of North America. It is mostly a solitary bird except during the mating season when it is more social. It is also one of the largest wading birds.

During the mating season, great blue herons nest in tall trees, rookeries, rock ledges, sea cliffs and even on the ground. Breeding adults are the most colorful, and both males and females look alike. Males bring sticks and twigs to the female, and she builds a flimsy nest for the eggs. Parents take turns sitting on the eggs. When the squabs are born, both parents help to feed their young.

Usually two-thirds of the heron's diet consists of small fish. They also eat snakes, small rodents, other water animals, lizards, frogs, and insects.

Reddish Egrets

Reddish egrets belong to the heron family and are a lot of fun to watch. In this picture, one of the egrets has its own fishing spot and chases the other reddish egret away. It doesn't mind that the brown pelican and other birds are close, but instead sprints frantically after its own kind. The egrets flap their wings in all directions as they race down the beach—one after the other.

Strictly a salt water bird, the reddish egret sports a pink pointy bill, rusty reddish head and neck and a grey-blue body, legs and feet. In an amusing way of quick movements, it wades in shallow water stirring up fish and other sea creatures with its feet so it can jump around catching them in its mouth!

Wood Storks

Wood storks will only reproduce when an adequate supply of food is available. If all is right for the wood stork, the male and the female build a nest together. They also share the responsibility of sitting on the eggs.

After the chicks are born, parents will catch and feed each young wood stork about 50 pounds of fish during their life in the nest. Young live in the nest for about 50 days.

The wood stork is the only native American stork and is considered one of the most endangered North American species. The loss of nesting sites, drainage and lowering water tables in Florida hurt the wood stork population. Droughts and the drying of feeding areas has also contributed to this problem. Many have concern for this bird of North America.

Snowy Egret

This snowy egret submerges its whole body in the pond, either hoping to spear a fish or perhaps just taking a bath. When it comes up from underneath the water, it shakes its wings and body to remove the water. After just a few seconds, the bird goes back to wading in more shallow water.

Usually, snowy egrets walk in shallow water—wiggling, probing or raking with one foot while balancing on the other. These actions often startle frogs and fish into motion. Egrets see this and spear the animal with their long bill. With their best foot forward, they're likely to get a meal.

Chuckwalla

A hungry chuckwalla extends its bright red tongue to eat some leaves from a desert plant. Chuckwallas are the second largest lizard in the United States and Canada, measuring about 16 inches long. They enjoy eating flowers and fruit from cactus. This one was photographed at the bottom of the Grand Canyon along the Colorado River.

Chuckwallas are generally afraid of people and hide in rock cracks. By puffing up its body, it fills up the crack so it is hard to get out. Native Americans used to eat them as a special food.

Lizard

Once during the Earth's history there was an Age of Reptiles. Gigantic creatures moved in the swamps and on the land. It was the Age of the Dinosaurs. The reptiles of today are mere leftovers of the ancient kinds. Lizards are one type of reptile whose fossils have been found in rocks formed during the time of the dinosaurs.

A small, harmless lizard with a red and yellow throat skin lives in my backyard. He is interesting to watch as he extends his throat to scare off other male lizards. He eats insects and spiders, and is only about five inches long. Once he lost his tail in a fight with a larger animal that wanted to eat him. After a few weeks, he started to grow a new tail.

Hummingbird

Almost everything about hummingbirds is unusual. They are the smallest birds in the world. They have iridescent, brightly colored feathers. They live in almost all climates and altitudes. They are swift in flight with wings that beat almost 100 times per second. They are capable of darting, mid-air stops and starts, hovering, flying backwards, sideways and straight up and down. They deserve the title "aerial masters" of the Earth.

Because of their size and speed, hummingbirds are rarely caught by birds of prey. Males are larger than females in the larger species, but females are larger than males in the smaller species. Males are more brightly colored in most species. There are at least 319 species of hummingbirds in the world.

Human Beings

Human beings are animals. Our brains are our greatest asset. Over thousands of years of evolution, some human beings have developed "brain and soul thinking." This is responsible thinking about the big picture of all life and our responsibility to the Earth. Brain and soul thinking is called wisdom. Humans with wisdom, instead of people with brains but no soul, need to lead others.

INDEX

Lorraine Salem Tufts is an internationally recognized author and wildlife photographer. She is the creator of the *Secrets in . . .* series of books. **Animals in Action** is her first effort for children. Ms. Tufts lives in the Rocky Mountains and Florida when she is not on assignment.

Order Form

Animals in Action
    1. Hardcover $15.95 x _____ (quantity) = _____

Shipping & Handling for 1 book
        Within the U.S. $4.00   _____
        Outside the U.S. $9.00   _____

Secrets in Yellowstone & Grand Teton National Parks
    2. Hardcover $29.95 x _____ (quantity) = _____
    3. Softcover $19.95 x _____ (quantity) = _____

Secrets in the Grand Canyon, Zion and Bryce Canyon National Parks
    4. Hardcover $29.95 x _____ (quantity) = _____
    5. Softcover $19.95 x _____ (quantity) = _____

Each additional book add $1.00 x _____ = _____
Add 6% sales tax for Florida shipments: _____
                    Total due _____

☐ **Please advise me of future publications**

Purchaser _____
Address _____
City _____ State _____ Zip _____
Phone (____) _____

☐ **Ship to (if different than above)**

Name _____
Address _____
City _____ State _____ Zip _____
(Please enclose check or money orders)

National Photographic Collections
P.O. Box 31355
Palm Beach Gardens, FL 33410-7355

NATIONAL PHOTOGRAPHIC COLLECTIONS

- -

Order Form

Animals in Action
    1. Hardcover $15.95 x _____ (quantity) = _____

Shipping & Handling for 1 book
        Within the U.S. $4.00   _____
        Outside the U.S. $9.00   _____

Secrets in Yellowstone & Grand Teton National Parks
    2. Hardcover $29.95 x _____ (quantity) = _____
    3. Softcover $19.95 x _____ (quantity) = _____

Secrets in the Grand Canyon, Zion and Bryce Canyon National Parks
    4. Hardcover $29.95 x _____ (quantity) = _____
    5. Softcover $19.95 x _____ (quantity) = _____

Each additional book add $1.00 x _____ = _____
Add 6% sales tax for Florida shipments: _____
                    Total due _____

☐ **Please advise me of future publications**

Purchaser _____
Address _____
City _____ State _____ Zip _____
Phone (____) _____

☐ **Ship to (if different than above)**

Name _____
Address _____
City _____ State _____ Zip _____
(Please enclose check or money orders)

National Photographic Collections
P.O. Box 31355
Palm Beach Gardens, FL 33410-7355

NATIONAL PHOTOGRAPHIC COLLECTIONS